W9-AUI-774

Safari Animals™
Animales de safari™

HYENAS

HIENAS

Maddie Gibbs

Traducción al español: Eduardo Alamán

PowerKiDS
press™

New York

Published in 2011 by The Rosen Publishing Group, Inc.
29 East 21st Street, New York, NY 10010

Copyright © 2011 by The Rosen Publishing Group, Inc.

First Edition

Editor: Amelie von Zumbusch
Layout Design: Greg Tucker

Traducción al español: Eduardo Alamán

Photo Credits: Cover, pp. 9, 17, 21, 24 (top left) Shutterstock.com; pp. 5, 13 Hemera/Thinkstock; pp. 7, 11, 23, 24 (bottom left, bottom right) iStockphoto/Thinkstock; pp. 15, 19, 24 (top right) Anup Shah/Photodisc/Thinkstock.

Library of Congress Cataloging-in-Publication Data

Gibbs, Maddie.
[Hyenas. Spanish & English]
Hyenas = Hienas / by Maddie Gibbs. — 1st ed.
    p. cm. — (Safari animals = Animales de safari)
Includes index.
ISBN 978-1-4488-3120-3 (library binding)
1. Hyenas—Juvenile literature. I. Title. II. Title: Hienas.
QL737.C24G5318 2011
599.74'3—dc22

2010020817

Manufactured in the United States of America

CPSIA Compliance Information: Batch #WW11PK: For Further Information contact Rosen Publishing, New York, New York at 1-800-237-9932

Web Sites: Due to the changing nature of Internet links, PowerKids Press has developed an online list of Web sites related to the subject of this book. This site is updated regularly. Please use this link to access the list: www.powerkidslinks.com/safari/hyenas/

CONTENTS

CONTENIDO

Hyenas are strong animals. They are smart, too.

Las hienas son animales muy fuertes. Además, las hienas son muy inteligentes.

Hyenas have sharp teeth. They have very strong **jaws**.

Las hienas tienen dientes filosos. Además, las hienas tienen **mandíbulas** fuertes.

Hyenas have big ears. This helps them hear well. They also have a good sense of smell.

Las hienas tienen orejas muy grandes. Esto les ayuda a oír muy bien. Además, las hienas tienen buen olfato.

Several kinds of hyenas live on Africa's **savannas**.

Muchos tipos de hienas viven en la **sabana** africana.

11

This is a spotted hyena.
Spotted hyenas are the largest
kind of hyena.

Ésta es una hiena manchada.
Las hienas manchadas son las
hienas más comunes.

13

Spotted hyenas are known for making a loud cry that sounds like laughter.

A las hienas manchadas se les conoce por un fuerte chillido que suena como una carcajada.

15

Spotted hyenas live in groups, called **clans**.

Las hienas manchadas viven en grupos llamados **manadas**.

Baby hyenas are called **cubs**. At first, cubs drink their mothers' milk. Later, they eat meat.

Las hienas bebé se llaman **cachorros**. De pequeños, los cachorros beben leche de sus mamás. Cuando crecen comen carne.

Hyenas are good hunters. They eat many kinds of animals.

Las hienas son buenas cazadoras. Las hienas comen muchos tipos de animales.

21

Hyenas also steal kills
from other animals.
They eat dead
animals they find, too.

Las hienas también
roban las presas
de otros animales.
Además, comen
animales muertos.

23

Words to Know / Palabras que debes saber

clan / (la) manada

cubs / (los) cachorros

jaws / (las) mandíbulas

savanna / (la) sabana